7/22/15

Carmelo Anthony

by Marty Gitlin

Consultant: Jon Krawczynski
AP Basketball Writer

BEARPORT
PUBLISHING

New York, New York

Credits

Cover and Title Page, © Bill Kostroun/AP Images, Michael Dwyer/AP Images, and John Bazemore/AP Images; 4, © Charles Krupa/AP Images; 5, © Charles Krupa/AP Images; 6, © Yearbook Library; 7, © Image of Sport; 8, © Michael Conroy/AP Images; 9, © Michael Conroy/AP Images; 10, © Tony Dejak/AP Images; 11, © Sue Ogrocki/AP Images; 12, © Kathy Willens/AP Images; 13, © John Bazemore/AP Images; 14, © WENN Photos/Newscom; 15, © Bebeto Matthews/AP Images; 16, © Steve Ruark/AP Images; 17, © Mitchell Layton/NBAE via Getty Images; 18, © Shutterstock; 19, © Sue Ogrocki/AP Images; 20, © Bebeto Matthews/AP Images; 21, © Bill Kostroun/AP Images; 22, © Michael Conroy/AP Images; 22, © Staff/MCT/Newscom.

Publisher: Kenn Goin
Senior Editor: Joyce Tavolacci
Creative Director: Spencer Brinker
Photo Researcher: Chrös McDougall

Library of Congress Cataloging-in-Publication Data

Gitlin, Marty.
  Carmelo Anthony / by Marty Gitlin.
    pages cm.—(Basketball heroes making a difference)
  Includes bibliographical references and index.
  ISBN 978-1-62724-546-3 (library binding)—ISBN 1-62724-546-4 (library binding)
  1. Anthony, Carmelo, 1984—Juvenile literature. 2. Basketball players—United States—Biography—Juvenile literature. 3. Generosity—Juvenile literature. I. Title.
  GV884.A58G57 2015
  796.323092—dc23
  [B]
                                    2014034563

For more information, write to Bearport Publishing Company, Inc., 45 West 21st Street, Suite 3B, New York, New York 10010. Printed in the United States of America.

10 9 8 7 6 5 4 3 2 1

Contents

Hero on the Court

It was Game 6 of the first round of the 2013 **NBA playoffs**, and the New York Knicks were in big trouble. Earlier in the game, the Knicks held a 24-point lead over the Boston Celtics. However, with less than five minutes left in the game, that lead had shrunk to just four points. It was time for the Knicks' superstar player, Carmelo Anthony, to step up.

Carmelo leaped into the air and made a **jumper**. A minute later, he fired a **three-pointer**. *Swish!* It sunk into the basket. New York went on to win 88–80. Carmelo had helped the Knicks win a playoff series for the first time since the year 2000!

Carmelo (left) rises above a Celtics defender to shoot.

4

Carmelo (right) led the Knicks with 21 points during Game 6 against the Celtics.

Carmelo is such a skilled shooter that he made more than 150 shots from beyond the three-point line in the 2012–2013 and 2013–2014 seasons.

A Challenging Start

Carmelo's path to NBA stardom had a rough start. Carmelo Kyam Anthony was born on May 29, 1984, in Brooklyn, New York. When Carmelo turned eight, his family moved to Baltimore, Maryland. Life in Baltimore wasn't easy. Not far from Carmelo's new home, people sold drugs and fights broke out. Luckily, playing basketball helped keep Carmelo out of trouble.

By high school, Carmelo's dunking and shooting skills had made him well known in the city. Soon, he became one of the best high school players in the country. However, his ball playing was much better than his schoolwork. To get into college, Carmelo knew he would also need to be a good student. As a result, he switched to a high school with a stronger **academic** program. His grades soon improved. Carmelo was now ready for the next step in his basketball career.

Carmelo attended Towson Catholic High School through his junior year.

Carmelo spent his senior year at Oak Hill Academy, a school known for both its basketball and academics.

Carmelo grew five inches (12.7 cm) by his sophomore year of high school. The extra height allowed him to change positions from **guard** to **forward**.

National Champ

After high school, Carmelo decided to play basketball for Syracuse University in New York. The Syracuse team had many talented young players, but Carmelo stood out. The six-foot-eight-inch (2 m) forward could soar through the air for dunks. Yet Carmelo also had a great jump shot and could make baskets from as far back as the three-point line. Jim Boeheim, Carmelo's coach at Syracuse, said that he was "by far, the best player in college basketball." In the **NCAA Tournament**, Carmelo played with the confidence of a more experienced player, leading his team to the national championship. He was then named Most Outstanding Player of the **Final Four**.

Carmelo averaged 22.2 points per game as a freshman at Syracuse in 2003.

Carmelo celebrates during the 2003 NCAA championship game against the University of Kansas.

Carmelo's height and jumping ability helped him get a lot of **rebounds**. He averaged 10.0 rebounds per game in the 2002–2003 season, leading all other college freshmen players.

NBA Time

After just one season at Syracuse, Carmelo felt he had improved enough to play in the NBA. The Denver Nuggets chose him third overall in the 2003 NBA **draft**. Unfortunately for Carmelo, the Nuggets had one of the worst records in the 2002–2003 season. Carmelo would have his work cut out for him. Yet he was up for the challenge.

Despite being a **rookie**, Carmelo showed that he was not intimidated by older and more experienced players. He soon became the Nuggets' leading scorer and quickly led the team to the playoffs. After that, Carmelo's great playing continued. Year after year, he averaged at least 20 points per game. With Carmelo leading the way, the Nuggets made the playoffs in each of the next six seasons.

Carmelo (left) and LeBron James (right) during a 2003 game

The Nuggets won just 17 games in the 2002–2003 season. One year later, after Carmelo joined their team, they won 43 games.

Carmelo averaged 28.9 points per game in the 2006–2007 season.

Big Star in New York

After playing for the Nuggets for seven seasons, Carmelo was ready for a change. He wanted to play closer to New York, where he had spent his early childhood. The Nuggets knew he wouldn't **re-sign**. So they traded him to the New York Knicks on February 22, 2011.

Carmelo was happy to be back in the state where he was born. Knicks fans were happy to have him, too. The team had struggled to win games in recent years. They hoped Carmelo would give the team the boost it needed. Once again, Carmelo dazzled fans with his shooting and dunking skills. That season, he scored an amazing 26.3 points per game. That scoring helped the Knicks qualify for the playoffs for the first time in seven seasons!

Carmelo celebrating during the 2011–2012 season opener

Carmelo dribbles down the court during a 2014 game with the Knicks.

No NBA player averaged more playing time in the 2013–2014 season than Carmelo's 38.7 minutes per game.

Starting a Foundation

Being a successful pro basketball player has allowed Carmelo to lead a very comfortable life. Yet he has never forgotten his early struggles when his family didn't have much money. So Carmelo decided to use his success to help those in need. In 2005, he started the Carmelo Anthony **Foundation**.

The foundation helps people living in poor communities through a number of different programs. For example, some programs provide food to people who are hungry. Others provide after-school activities for kids. Carmelo is especially passionate about helping children. He hopes his work will inspire kids growing up in poor areas to go after their goals. "Nobody should expect more of you than you expect of yourself," Carmelo says.

Carmelo cuts a ribbon to celebrate the opening of a new basketball court built by his foundation in Puerto Rico in 2014.

The Carmelo Anthony Foundation runs its own **charity** programs. It also **donates** money to other organizations such as the Living Classrooms Foundation in Baltimore.

Carmelo helps distribute food in Brooklyn in 2011. His foundation organized the event alongside Feed the Children and the Boys & Girls Club of America.

Hometown Hero

Carmelo has helped kids throughout the United States and Puerto Rico. Yet he feels a special bond with the children of Baltimore. "That's the city that raised me," he has said.

Many kids in the poorer parts of Baltimore do not have a lot of opportunities outside of school. In response, Carmelo donated $1.5 million to help create the Carmelo Anthony Youth Development Center in East Baltimore. The huge 33,000 square-foot (3,066 sq m) center, built in 2006, offers many programs for kids. Some are just for fun, like sports, games, and art activities. However, other programs help kids with schoolwork and teach them about health, life skills, and finding jobs when they're older.

Carmelo takes a break to talk with a young fan during a charity basketball game he hosted in Baltimore.

Every year, Carmelo's foundation looks for 250 middle school students who work hard to improve their communities or help their families. Carmelo then meets with them as part of his "Be More" program.

Carmelo talks to kids at the grand opening of the Carmelo Anthony Youth Development Center in Baltimore in 2006.

Saving Animals

Carmelo doesn't just help people with his work off the court. He also reaches out to animals in need. The Knicks' superstar loves animals, especially tigers. So he was inspired to join forces with WildAid, a group that works to save certain animals from becoming **extinct**.

How do Carmelo and WildAid help? Some animals, such as tigers and rhinoceroses, are **endangered**. Yet, even though they are in danger of dying out, these animals are still being hunted illegally. Carmelo has starred in television ads for WildAid to raise awareness of this problem. The ads call attention to the importance of stopping the illegal hunting.

Without a stop to illegal hunting, animals such as tigers could become extinct.

Carmelo and LeBron James (left)

Carmelo is a close friend of Cleveland Cavaliers superstar LeBron James. Carmelo and LeBron have taken part in each other's charity events.

Helping in a Crisis

Before moving to Baltimore as a child, Carmelo lived in the Red Hook neighborhood of Brooklyn. In October 2012, a powerful hurricane hit the East Coast of the United States. It flooded areas of New York and New Jersey and left millions without electricity. Four days after the terrible storm, Carmelo showed up in Brooklyn to help.

At that very difficult time, Carmelo's foundation teamed up with two other organizations to provide 500 boxes filled with food and household supplies to the people of Red Hook. "I have no power, no heat, and I was running out of clean clothes," one resident said. "This is a great relief." Carmelo once again showed that as much as he is a hero to his cheering fans, he is an even bigger hero to those in need.

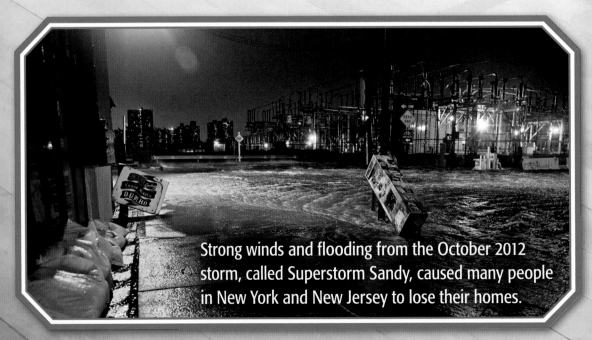

Strong winds and flooding from the October 2012 storm, called Superstorm Sandy, caused many people in New York and New Jersey to lose their homes.

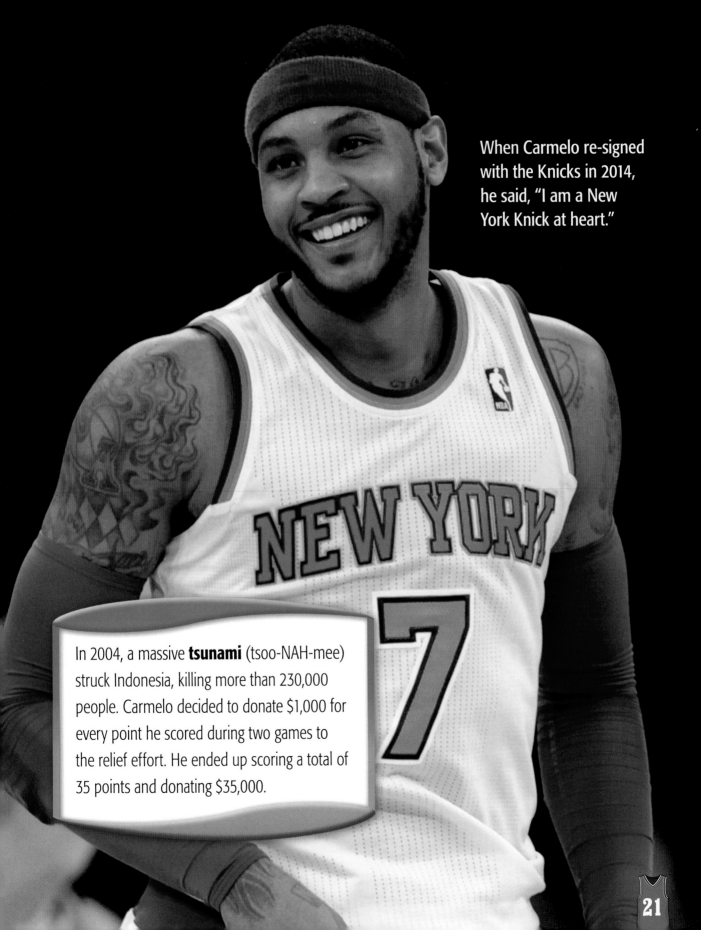

When Carmelo re-signed with the Knicks in 2014, he said, "I am a New York Knick at heart."

In 2004, a massive **tsunami** (tsoo-NAH-mee) struck Indonesia, killing more than 230,000 people. Carmelo decided to donate $1,000 for every point he scored during two games to the relief effort. He ended up scoring a total of 35 points and donating $35,000.

The Carmelo File

Carmelo is a basketball hero on and off the court. Here are some highlights.

Carmelo never stopped appreciating the importance of education after joining the NBA. In 2007, he donated $3 million to Syracuse University. That allowed Syracuse to build a basketball practice center. The school named the new building the Carmelo K. Anthony Basketball Center.

Carmelo's fans often call him by his nickname, *Melo*.

Carmelo made history on January 24, 2014, when he made 23 out of 35 shots to score 62 points against the Charlotte Bobcats. No Knicks player had ever scored more points in a single game. Carmelo also made all ten free throws he attempted during the game.

Glossary

academic (ak-uh-DEM-ik) relating to studying or learning

charity (CHA-ruh-tee) a group that tries to help people in need

donates (DOH-nayts) gives something to a cause

draft (DRAFT) an event in which professional teams take turns choosing new athletes to play for them

endangered (en-DAYN-jurd) at risk of dying out

extinct (ek-STINGKT) no longer existing

Final Four (FYE-nuhl FOR) the semifinals of the NCAA college basketball championships; the stage of the basketball tournament where only four teams remain in competition

forward (FOR-wurd) one of the standard positions on a basketball team; the player is often responsible for much of the team's scoring

foundation (foun-DAY-shuhn) an organization set up to help or give money to worthwhile causes

guard (GARD) one of the standard positions on a basketball team; a team's two guards are responsible for taking longer distance shots

jumper (JUHMP-ur) a jump shot; a shot taken by a player while jumping

NBA (EN-BEE-AY) letters standing for the National Basketball Association, the professional men's basketball league in North America

NCAA Tournament (EN-SEE-AY-AY TUR-nuh-muhnt) college basketball's yearly series of games that result in one team becoming the champion

playoffs (PLAY-awfss) a series of games that determine which teams will play in a championship

rebounds (REE-boundz) balls that are caught by a player after a missed shot

re-sign (ree-SINE) to agree to play for a team for an added period of time

rookie (RUK-ee) a first-year player

three-pointer (three-POINT-ur) a long-distance shot that is worth three points rather than two

tsunami (tsoo-NAH-mee) a huge ocean wave or group of waves that causes great flooding and damage

Bibliography

Begley, Ian. "Carmelo Anthony Delivers Supplies." ESPN.com (November 9, 2012).

Kartalija, Jessica. "Carmelo Is Making Moves in the Court & in the Community." CBS Baltimore (February 23, 2011).

Spears, Mark J. "Melo to Donate Millions to 'Cuse." *The Denver Post* (November 8, 2006).

www.thisismelo.com/foundation/about

Read More

Fishman, Jon M. *Carmelo Anthony (Amazing Athletes).* Minneapolis, MN: Lerner (2014).

MacRae, Sloan. *Carmelo Anthony (Sports Heroes).* New York: Rosen (2012).

Torres, John. *Carmelo Anthony.* Newark, DE: Mitchell Lane (2013).

Learn More Online

To learn more about Carmelo Anthony and the New York Knicks, visit **www.bearportpublishing.com/BasketballHeroes**

Index

Louisburg Library
Bringing People and Information Together